I0801969

IMAGES
of America

NORTH DAKOTA RODEO

ON THE COVER: This photograph is of Dean Armstrong, a member of the North Dakota Six Pack, riding famed Figure Four at the 1956 Dickinson Match of Champions. (Osborn's Studio.)

IMAGES
of America

NORTH DAKOTA RODEO

Cathy A. Langemo

ARCADIA
PUBLISHING

ISBN 978-0-7385-8253-5

Published by Arcadia Publishing
Charleston, South Carolina

Printed in the United States of America

Library of Congress Control Number: 2011928974

For all general information, please contact Arcadia Publishing:
Telephone 843-853-2070
Fax 843-853-0044
E-mail sales@arcadiapublishing.com
For customer service and orders:
Toll-Free 1-888-313-2665

Visit us on the Internet at www.arcadiapublishing.com

This book is dedicated not only to the cowboys and cowgirls, past and present, but also to everyone who makes the spectator's rodeo experience great.

Contents

FOREWORD

Open the chute gate. Here comes Cathy Langemo with another great look at life on the plains of North Dakota.

Cathy, who has written four books and edited countless others, now takes us on a trip through cowboy country with a look at the sport of rodeo. Rodeo, America's original sport, has a long and colorful history on the grasslands from Texas to Canada.

Rodeos began in the 1800s as a way for cowboys to test their skills against one another. The sport has evolved into a multimillion-dollar business pitting contestant against contestant, rider against animal. However, cowboys and cowgirls do not always see much of the money. They travel at their own expense, pay entry fees, and walk away empty handed, or they leave with a check if they drew a good ride, became poetry in motion, and made the whistle.

North Dakota features one of the nation's oldest continuous rodeos—the famous Mandan Rodeo, where they have been riding broncs since 1882. Rodeos also define a community or a cause. The reservation community of Sanish is underwater, but it is remembered for its memorable rodeos of the late 1940s and early 1950s.

The Dickinson Match of Champions is long gone, but people still talk about the incredible rides by the rodeo greats—Casey Tibbs, Dean Armstrong, and Joe Chase. In Killdeer, rodeo defines the community and, at the Home On The Range, the world series of bronc riding takes place the first weekend in August each year.

Join Cathy as she explores the great rodeos of North Dakota and the riders, horses, and bulls that have become legends. *North Dakota Rodeo* is a great ride and a good read by a writer who has researched the sport of rodeo and knows that eight seconds can be an eternity.

—Darrell Dorgan, executive director
North Dakota Cowboy Hall of Fame

ACKNOWLEDGMENTS

Many thanks to all who assisted in the production of this book, including Arcadia Publishing employees for their assistance, advice, reminders, encouragement, and patience; the North Dakota Cowboy Hall of Fame for use of photographic and biographical collections; North Dakota Cowboy Hall of Fame staff, including Darrell Dorgan, Kathy Miller, and NDCHF board president and rodeo historian Phil Baird for their research assistance and review of photograph identifications and text; and all who were interested in this project and encouraged me along the way.

Lastly, and most importantly, I publicly thank my son, Barrett Langemo, and his family for their willingness to be ignored for days at a time while I was working on this and many other special projects.

Unless otherwise noted, all photographs are credited to the North Dakota Cowboy Hall of Fame or belong to the North Dakota Cowboy Hall of Fame.

The following abbreviations are used throughout this book:
NDCHF—North Dakota Cowboy Hall of Fame
NDRA—North Dakota Rodeo Association
RAA—Rodeo Association of America
RCA—Rodeo Cowboys Association (formerly Cowboys Turtle Association)
PRCA—Professional Rodeo Cowboys Association
PBR—Professional Bull Riders
GPIRA—Great Plains Indian Rodeo Association
INFR—Indian National Finals Rodeo
NDHSRA—North Dakota High School Rodeo Association
NHSRA—National High School Rodeo Association
NFR—National Finals Rodeo (now known as Wrangler NFR or WNFR)
ACRA—American Collegiate Rodeo Association
NIRA—National Intercollegiate Rodeo Association

Introduction

Rodeo, a truly American sport, was not always the well-organized, smoothly operating event that cowboys and cowgirls participate in and that rodeo fans enjoy today. Not originally a sporting event, it was an integral part of cattle ranching in Spanish areas, where the cowboys were called vaqueros.

The earliest rodeo events were Sunday afternoons spent with cowboys competing against each other in the usual ranch activities: bronc breaking, roping, and team penning. The afternoons of competition and fun were a break from the hard work they did all week long.

In time, the gathering of cowboys during roundups and brandings and on Sunday afternoons brought about competitive matches of the best cowboys. And, over the years, a uniform set of rules came about with the organization of the Rodeo Association of America, Cowboys Turtle Association, Rodeo Cowboys Association and Professional Rodeo Cowboys Association.

Cowgirls once rode in all rodeo events, including rough stock, at pre–World War II rodeos. After the war, they formed the Women's Professional Rodeo Association, giving them the opportunity to compete in sanctioned contests at PRCA rodeos and in rough stock and roping events at all-girl rodeos.

The rodeo association rules were used throughout the United Sates and Canada, and a point-award system helped determine the world champions in each event. The money won during the season counts in the association's total point systems. Along with the champion in each event, an all-around championship is won by the cowboy or cowgirl who earns the highest total points in several events.

Today, the point system determines the qualifiers for national finals and the standings for world championships.

One

Mandan Rodeo

In this photograph is Lawrence "Gene" Pedersen on Leo Cremer's bronc at the c. 1941 Mandan Rodeo. The Mandan Rodeo, promoted as the longest continually running rodeo in the country, began in 1882 and became part of the North Dakota State Fair in 1897. It was a very popular event in the area, so much so that it went on during World War I and welcomed home troops in 1919.

In this photograph is a pre-1932 Mandan Rodeo event. There were Native American exhibits, regalia, dancing, and drumming at the fair and at the Mandan Rodeo, which later became known as the Fourth of July Mandan Jaycees Rodeo. The Mandan Rodeo was inducted into the NDCHF in 2006.

Pictured is an unidentified bronc rider at a Mandan Rodeo. The rodeo offers several performances from July 2–4 each year. This was formerly at the rodeo grounds in south Mandan, where the rodeo was held for 110 years. Since 1990, the rodeo has been held at the Dacotah Centennial Park on the Strip between Mandan and Bismarck. (Doubleday photograph.)

This unidentified rodeo star is looking for a soft landing. The Mandan Rodeo was one of the main events on the "Cowboy Christmas" circuit because of the quality of rough stock and the amount of potential prize money. Rodeo participants could travel to several rodeos over the Fourth of July holiday. (Doubleday photograph.)

Emanuel Chase, of Halliday, is pictured at a Mandan Rodeo. He built rodeo arenas on the Fort Berthold Reservation for young cowboys to practice. Chase helped put on the first matched bronc riding at Sanish. He competed in calf-roping and bareback- and saddle-bronc riding. His early death in 1951 was a great loss to North Dakota rodeo.

Marge Greenough, on Boxer, is pictured at a Mandan Rodeo. During the 1930s, Greenough and her sister Alice participated in most of the main rodeo events throughout the United States, including at Madison Square Garden, and in foreign countries. They were bronc riders until 1941, when girls' bronc riding ceased, resulting in the end of their rodeo careers. Greenough was also a journalist and a movie and television star. (Doubleday photograph.)

This is a photograph of a wild Brahma bull riding at a Mandan Rodeo. The cowboy needs to stay on the bull for at least eight seconds for a successful ride. The more spurring the rider does, and the more the bull bucks, the better his score. (Doubleday photograph.)

Ed Orgaard tries out a Mandan Rodeo steer. If the rider holds on until the buzzer goes, he can earn a score. The judges can credit 50 points for the animal's performance and 50 for the rider's performance, making a potential total of 100 points.

The photograph shows Lawrence "Gene" Pedersen in a steer-wrestling event at a July 1947 Mandan Rodeo. The hazer for the ride was Abe Graham, and the steer was from stock contractor Leo Cremer. Hazing is key to a successful run, as the hazer's job is to keep the steer going straight.

The saddle-bronc rider is trying hard to keep from being bucked off Sure Shot at a Mandan Rodeo. If bucked off, all he gets for his effort is a cheer from the rodeo crowd, as there is no money if the rider does not make the required time. (Doubleday photograph.)

This cowboy gives his best to stay on bareback bronc Timbuck Too at a Mandan Rodeo, but he misses the eight seconds. Sometimes, a rider travels many miles for a chance to stay on a bucking bronc until the buzzer. The match of the rider and the horse makes all of the difference.

Saddle-bronc rider Ken Kruger is bucked off the bronc Hippy at a Mandan Rodeo. Rodeo is a gamble—sometimes the cowboy makes the whistle, sometimes not. Sometimes he goes home with winnings and sometimes empty-handed. (Doubleday photograph.)

This c. 1927 photograph is of Joe Wicks on Bite 'Em at a Mandan Rodeo. He began his rodeo career on the Steve Weekes ranch in 1916. Known as "the Heart River Kid," he was an outstanding saddle-bronc rider. He also rode bareback broncs and steers. Wicks participated in western North Dakota rodeos as one of the state's leading saddle-bronc cowboys. He also performed as a rodeo clown and a rodeo producer.

Reuben DeCamp, of Fort Clark and Morton County, rides Leave Me with the Smile at the 1925 Mandan Rodeo. DeCamp competed in the second annual roundup held at the Weekes ranch over the Fourth of July holiday in 1924 and in the Mandan Roundup in 1925 and 1926. He also competed at rodeos in Almont, Carson, Sanish, and Yucca. (Photograph by Poague, *Minneapolis Journal*.)

This photograph shows a specialty act during intermission at a Mandan Rodeo. The Mandan Rodeo Association, headed by Frank Wetzstein and a committee of Mandan businessmen, reenergized the rodeo during the 1940s and early 1950s, bringing in entertainers like Gene Autry, Rex Allen, and the Sons of the Pioneers. (Lee Mohr photograph.)

A rodeo clown rides on a donkey during a local rodeo. A rodeo is never quite complete without entertainment, whether it is clowns, trick riders, or cowboys performing rope tricks. (Lee Mohr photograph.)

This cowboy did not quite make the eight seconds at this rodeo. Eight seconds are key to a successful ride in the rough-stock events, including bareback-bronc and bull riding. (Lee Mohr photograph.)

A bareback-bronc cowboy holds on tight to the rope for a great ride at a Mandan Rodeo. The spectators get most excited during rides when both the rider and animal give it their all. (Lee Mohr photograph.)

This cowboy shows off his trick-roping skills at a Mandan Rodeo. This is just one form of rodeo entertainment that takes place during the breaks between events. Others are chuckwagon races, trick riding, and wild-cow milking. (Lee Mohr photograph.)

Delvin Reich, a pro-rodeo and all-around hand, is shown on Fettig's Steel Dust at the 1967 Mandan Rodeo. He rodeoed in the RCA and the PRCA, claiming his first saddle-bronc title in 1959. Reich's NDRA state championships included five RCA bareback-, four saddle-bronc, three steer-wrestling, and three all-around championships. He also competed in bull riding for four years. (Rabun photograph.)

This cowboy works hard to stay on his bronc. In the early 1970s, stock for area rodeos was provided by the Figure Four Rodeo Company of Watford City, and in the late 1970s, it was provided by Figure Four, Joe Berger, George Bruington, and Jim Mosbrucker. Prize money by 1980 was over $20,000. (Lee Mohr photograph.)

The Mandan Rodeo is often referred to as one of the main events on the "Cowboy Christmas" circuit because of the quality rough stock and the amount of prize money offered. It was part of the "big loop" that included Cheyenne Frontier Days and the Calgary Stampede. (Lee Mohr photograph.)

One

KILLDEER MOUNTAINS ROUNDUP RODEO

The photograph above is of the Killdeer Mountains Roundup Rodeo in its early days. It is one of North Dakota's oldest professional sporting events, and it has contributed greatly to the preservation of North Dakota's Western culture and heritage. The brainchild of trail driver and rodeo producer Sam Rhoades, it began as part of the Dunn County Fair. The RCA sanctioned the event in 1949, and the last rodeo in the natural arena in the Killdeer Mountains was in 1954. (Leo Harris photograph.)

Ray Stiles rides Banjo String at the 1926 Killdeer Mountains Roundup Rodeo. The Killdeer Mountains Rodeo Association ran the rodeo from 1941 to 1946 when Matt Olson became the grounds owner and rodeo sponsor. During World War II, a shortage of gas and young cowboys forced the old timers to don their spurs and chaps to keep the tradition alive. The rodeo moved into Killdeer in 1955 and continues to be popular. (Leo Harris photograph.)

The Fettig Rodeo Company provided rodeo stock for many years and was well known for producing and providing stock for rodeos in the region and taking stock to the NFR. The pick-up men in this photograph are trying to get into place to catch the bronc rider at the Killdeer Rodeo. The Killdeer Mountains Roundup Rodeo celebrated its 75th anniversary in 1998.

The Killdeer Mountains Roundup Rodeo Quadrille team is shown at the 1944 rodeo. Members were John and Gloria Quilliam, Jim Bang, Doris Dullum, and Norman and Whitten Frerck. Quilliam started his rodeo career in 1919 and spurred wildly on bareback broncs for 16 years at local rodeos. He partnered with Louie Pelissier and Gene McCormick in the 1950s and 1960s and, with McCormick, won the team roping in 1963. In 1962, the event was promoted as "North Dakota's largest world championship rodeo."

The Killdeer Saddle Club began sponsoring the rodeo around 1966 and continues to do so today. It has been under the direction of five presidents: Peg O'Neil, Cleo Veeder, Thorris Sandvick, Tex

Appledoorn, and Bob Kleeman. The Killdeer Mountains Roundup Rodeo brought out a large crowd for the 75th anniversary in 1998. The rodeo was also inducted into the NDCHF in 1998.

The audience is excited about the saddle-bronc ride, and they cheer on the rider. Over the years, the nation's finest cowboys and cowgirls have appeared in the rodeo's arena. In 1984, world champion calf roper Paul Tierney set a PRCA record with an amazing 6.9 seconds. Rodeo is about families, who bring their picnic lunches along and later dance the night away.

Three

Dickinson Match of Champions

The photograph shows Joe Chase on Jim Barnhart's No. 2 Whiz Bang at the August 12, 1956, Dickinson Match of Champions. In 1950, nine-time world champion Casey Tibbs of South Dakota won a special bareback match against Bill Linderman. The Dickinson Match of Champions, organized and promoted by Ray Schnell and his sons Raymond, Howard, and Willard, was held each August for 13 years at an arena southeast of Dickinson.

The Match of Champions started as an invitational calf-roping event in the summer 1946, with saddle-bronc riding added in 1948. The first "Match" featured North Dakota cowboys Jim, Tom, and Alvin Tescher and Dean Armstrong competing against Feek Tooke's broncs from Montana. Howard Schnell presents a buckle to Casey Tibbs, the winner of the 1955 Match. Tibbs went on to win four consecutive Matches (1953–1956) and nine RCA world championships.

Casey Tibbs, left, and Joe Chase visit with the crowd at the Dickinson Match of Champions. Tibbs won or tied for first in four consecutive Matches, tying with Chase in 1956. Chase, who later qualified for two NFRs, won the 1957 Match.

Bob Aber, of Beach, North Dakota, rides General Ike at the 1956 Match of Champions. Word spread fast, and soon the world's best were clamoring to face off against the best North Dakota riders. This is what brought the cowboys: the chance to climb on some of the best broncs around. For more than a decade, the world's top bronc riders came to Dickinson each August.

Harley May rides Old Fitzgerald at the 1956 Match. After the photograph was taken, May was thrown over the horse's head. Owner John Steen is to the right in the photograph. The top 15 bronc riders in the nation competed, including Casey Tibbs, Bill Linderman, Guy Weekes, Deb Copenhaver, Harley May, Bill Robinson, Bill Hancock, Jack Buschbom, and Alvin Nelson. Announcer James "Cy" Taillon kept the audience informed.

Bob Aber is on Crossroads at the 1957 Dickinson Match of Champions. The Match, often considered the world series of saddle-bronc riding, brought in some of the best bucking horses in the business, coming from the Tooke, Greenough, Orr, and Fettig strings.

Raymond Schnell (left) and Willard Schnell, organizers of the Match of Champions, are introduced at the Match. Only the world's best cowboys and livestock were invited to participate. The Schnells later added top rodeo animals from Jim Barnhart, John Steen, and Oral Zumwalt. The last Match of Champions, held in 1958, featured only bareback riding.

Howard Schnell participated in calf roping at the Dickinson Match of Champions. Ralph Klein topped the calf-roping event, and Emanuel Chase edged out South Dakotan Homer Stands in bronc riding. Stands took first in the bareback riding. After the 1958 Match, the famous arena was dismantled. The NDCHF inducted the event in 1999. (Osborn's Studio photograph.)

Four

Sanish Rodeo

The photograph above is a view of the Sanish Rodeo grounds. The town of Sanish, on the edge of one of the last big cattle ranges, was an ideal spot for developing a rodeo arena. In April 1947, a group of ranchers, farmers, and businessmen—all interested in growing the community and the great Western sport of rodeo—formed the Sanish Rodeo Association. (Leo Harris photograph.)

The first board of directors included Earl Nice, Brooks Keogh, Harry Mendenhall, Doug McGrady, Fred LaRocque, Royal Logan, E.A. McLaughlin, Sidney Benn, Wendell Van Dyke, and C.A.

Pickering. The corrals and arena were constructed southwest of the Old Sanish Bridge, and the first Sanish Rodeo was held July 3–5, 1947. (Osborn's Studio photograph.)

In 1948, the two large grandstands and the bowery were built. The first year, in 1947, $2,205 was offered in prizes. The rodeo soon became second in the state in the amount of prize money

paid out and second to none in the number of contestants and stock out of the chute each day. (Osborn's Studio photograph.)

The rodeo committee and rodeo participants joined the entry parade at each performance. By the early 1950s, the prize money grew to $3,600. Attendance also grew, with 10,292 admissions in 1949 and 20,000 in 1950. (Leo Harris photograph.)

Several Native Americans are pictured participating in the entry parade. Specialty acts were also featured at the Sanish Rodeo, including the famous three-horse Roman standing rider who performed a fire jump and the standing Roman jump on the backs of Brahma bulls.

The entry parade continues. Nearly everyone involved in the rodeo participated in the parade. The grand entry parade was lengthy, colorful, and included many Native Americans. (Leo Harris photograph.)

The colorful pageantry was an important part of the Sanish Rodeo. The Native American dancers provided entertainment during the rodeo. (Leo Harris photograph.)

The Native American drum group also played a big part in the opening of each Sanish Rodeo performance. Drum groups provided a sacred, spiritual side to the rodeo activities. (Leo Harris photograph.)

Hundreds of Native American families pitched tents below Mount Crow Flies High and wore their native feather and bead full-dress regalia during the three-day event. (Leo Harris photograph.)

The wild-cow rider did not quite make it to a score. Sanish Rodeo events included saddle-bronc and bareback riding, wild-horse races, bulldogging, calf roping, relay races, wild-cow milking, and Shetland pony races. Wild-cow riding at the Sanish Rodeo was an especially fun event. (Leo Harris photograph.)

This Sanish Rodeo saddle-bronc ride did not end quite like the rider had hoped. A head-first landing must have hurt because the Sanish arena was famous for "being hard." Many of the Sanish Rodeo riders were from the Fort Berthold Indian Reservation. (Leo Harris photograph.)

A bareback-bronc ride at the Sanish Rodeo is pictured here. As the photograph label reads, "Hook 'em, cowboy." (Leo Harris photograph.)

Harvey Grevious rides a bareback bronc at a Sanish Rodeo. Did he make the required 10 seconds? If so, he received a score from the judges. If not, there was no score for him this round. In the 1950s, the qualifying time for bareback was changed to eight seconds. (Leo Harris photograph.)

Bronc riders willingly match their skills against the bucking broncs at the Sanish Rodeo. The rider was fortunate to find a soft landing after the ride, as the horse attempts to avoid stepping on the downed rider. (Leo Harris photograph.)

This photograph reads that the saddle-bronc rider is "Reuben DeCamp." However, it cannot be him because the time frame is not accurate. DeCamp was no longer alive during the years that the Sanish Rodeo was operating. The identity of the rider is unknown. (Leo Harris photograph.)

This unidentified cowboy rides a saddle bronc at a Sanish Rodeo. (Leo Harris photograph.)

This photograph of a group of Sanish Rodeo cowboys includes, from left to right, Harry Beaks, Duane Charging, Emanuel Chase, Alvin Tescher, Jim Tescher, and Tom Tescher. Saddle-bronc winners at the 1948 Sanish Rodeo were Tom Tescher (first place), Jim Tescher (second place), and Alvin Tescher (third place).

An unidentified cowboy participates in the saddle-bronc event at a Sanish Rodeo. (Leo Harris photograph.)

An unidentified cowboy challenges a saddle bronc at the Sanish Rodeo. As is written on the photograph, "Let 'er buck." (Leo Harris photograph.)

A saddle bronc is giving his best bucks to get the cowboy off. Because of the inundation of the Sanish area after the Garrison Dam was built, the seventh and final Sanish Rodeo performances were held from July 3–5, 1953, with about 15,000 people attending. The rodeo had a short, but colorful, history that lives on in the memories of those who participated and attended. (Leo Harris.)

This bucking bronc is serious about his job. What a ride for this unidentified cowboy. Along with amazing livestock, the Sanish Rodeo also offered specialty acts to entertain the audience, and there were area bands that marched in the parades and performed concerts.

This cowboy is trying to make the eight-second saddle-bronc ride. The Sanish Rodeo operated for only seven years and, although short lived, it was very popular with the cowboys, cowgirls, and spectators who attended. The Sanish Rodeo was inducted into the NDCHF in 2011.

Five

Home On The Range Champions Ride

The Home On The Range Champions Ride, one of the nation's few remaining saddle-bronc matches, has been compared to baseball's all-star game—the best horses against the best cowboys. The Champions Ride was born when professional rodeo cowboys and brothers Jim and Tom Tescher proposed the match to help defray the costs of operating and upgrading the nonprofit organization.

The photograph above shows Dan Mortensen's ride, winner of the 1990 Champions Ride. The Home On The Range arena boasts natural hillside seating—Western, the way it used to be when the sport of rodeo was in its infancy. Cowboys enjoy the no-frills atmosphere of the Champions Ride, the rodeo spirit seems more alive, and the world-class bucking stock performs best at Home On The Range.

Robert Etbauer, reigning world champion saddle-bronc rider at that time, rode Papa Smurf of the Calgary Stampede rodeo string during the 1989 Champions Ride. Ray Schnell and his sons Raymond and Willard managed the event for many years, and Cy Taillon served as announcer. Taillon reported the scores made on stock provided by Harley Roth, Jim Madden, the Fettig Brothers, and John Steen. (Ray Erhardt photograph.)

Ty Murray, of Stephenville, Texas, scores 85 points on Scenic Site during the short-go at the Home On The Range Champions Ride. A partial list of Champions Ride winners reads like a who's who of rodeo—Alvin Nelson, Duane Howard, Pete Fredericks, Jim and Tom Tescher, Brad Gjermundson, Robert Etbauer, Dan Mortensen, and Ty Murray. (Ray Erhardt photograph.)

Steve Marchant, of Mud Butte, South Dakota, rides Yet Marvelous, the best bronc of the 1993 Champions Ride. For generations, families have been making the trip across North Dakota for an afternoon of bronc-riding action at the Home On The Range Champions Ride near Sentinel Butte.

Glen O'Neill, of Water Valley, Alberta, scores 88 points on Papa Smurf during the 1997 Home On The Range Champions Ride. The ranch itself, established in 1950 by Fr. Elwood Cassedy as a home for neglected and homeless boys, observed its 50th anniversary in 2000, the year it was inducted into the NDCHF.

The winner is Jeremy Crane of Bismarck. He rode Copenhagen, the best bronc of the 1998 Home On The Range Champions Ride. By invitation only, the best horses provided by stock contractors across North America challenge the top saddle-bronc cowboys. The first Champions Ride was won by Alvin Nelson.

Red Lemel, of Mud Butte, South Dakota, rides Warfare Rocket at the Champions Ride c. 1998. Running since 1957, the rodeo benefits the boys and girls living at Home On The Range. (Ray Erhardt photograph.)

Tom Reeves, of Eagle Butte, South Dakota, was the winner at the 2001 Home On The Range Champions Ride. The Champions Ride is exciting for participants and spectators because of the quality of the riders and stock. (Ray Erhardt photograph.)

Glen O'Neill, originally from Australia, rides Papa Smurf at the 2001 Champions Ride. Some say the Champions Ride is a preview of the Wrangler NFR, as many of the same broncs and cowboys go on to the WNFR in Las Vegas. (Ray Erhardt photograph.)

World champion saddle-bronc rider Brad Gjermundson challenges Papa Smurf at the Champions Ride. When asked why they come to the Champions Ride, the cowboys give two reasons: the horses and the kids. They appreciate the opportunity to draw famous saddle broncs, but they are also aware that their participation benefits the residents. Ultimately, it is the kids who win at this rodeo. (Ray Erhardt photograph.)

Five

Minot Y's Men's Rodeo

Jack Chase is pictured steer wrestling at the Minot Y's Men's Rodeo. Chase was a working cowboy on Standing Rock Indian Reservation ranches in the 1950s. He started traveling to rodeos in the 1940s, competing until 1980. The Minot Y's Men's Rodeo began in 1955, when North Dakota's first indoor rodeo was held in the new Minot City Auditorium. The rodeo celebrated its 50th anniversary in 2005.

This photograph was taken at the 40th anniversary of the Minot Y's Men's Rodeo in 1994. Included are some of the original contestants and the rodeo committee members. Pictured are, from left to right, (first row) Willard Schnell, Herb Parker, Orrin Baertsch, Ken Miller, and Bob Lowe; (second row) Paul Ristvedt, George Christensen, Frank Holbrook, Armand Haugstad, and Roger Herigstad.

Steer wrestling has been a popular event at the Minot rodeo. Since the rodeo's inception, the Y's men have volunteered time, talent, and financial resources to provide audiences with a quality show and competitors with an opportunity to further their careers. Competitors such as the Teschers, Hawkeye Henson, Ty Murray, and Jesse Bail have participated in the Y's Men's Rodeo.

A bull rider enjoys the excellent rough stock at the Minot rodeo. Note the clown in the barrel. He is protected yet ready to help if necessary. In 1955, Jerry Boren, Phil Fettig, and Willard Schnell suggested a Minot indoor rodeo; the Y's men immediately went to work, netting $900 the first year.

A barrel racer at the 1996 Minot Y's Men's Rodeo hopes for the fastest time. It was the first NDRA championship indoor rodeo, and it was approved by the RCA (now the PRCA). This was accomplished by using nationally recognized stock contractors, competitors, judges, rodeo queens, pick-up men, and barrelmen.

This unidentified bullfighter takes time during the Minot Y's Men's Rodeo to tease the bull. It can be very exciting for the spectators but very dangerous for the bullfighter. Strong national sponsorships, Wrangler bullfights, and a Wild West rodeo for special children with physical or mental challenges have been added to this rodeo.

This unidentified cowboy "goes out the back door" on a bucking bronc at the Minot Y's Men's Rodeo. The rodeo is special, as nearly all rodeo proceeds finance youth activities at the Minot family YMCA and Y camp, where thousands of children have experienced the horse master's program. To date, contributions to various projects exceed $1 million.

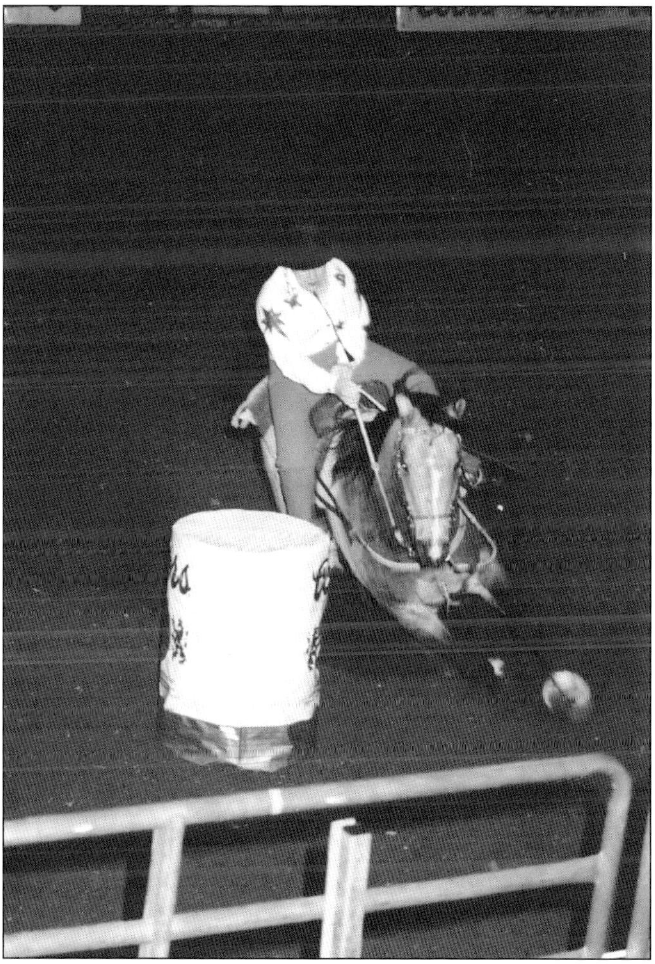

This bullfighter gets the bull's attention during a bull-riding event at the 1996 Minot Y's Men's Rodeo. The Pro-Rodeo Hall of Fame honored the Minot Y's Men's Rodeo, commemorating its more than 40 years as an RCA and PRCA–sanctioned event. It promotes Western culture, positively impacts Minot's economy, and gives PRCA contestants a chance to add to their winnings.

The unidentified barrel racer at the 1996 Minot Y's Men's Rodeo hopes that all of the barrels will be standing at the end of her run and that she has the fastest time of all the barrel racers.

The Minot Y's Men's Rodeo was inducted into the NDCHF in 2003. This photograph of the committee includes, from left to right, (first row) Travis Zablotney, Wayne Semrau, Dennis Nordquist, and Brian Pease; (second row) Lenny Behm, Daryle Ostdahl, Paul Christensen, Marv Semrau, Gov. John Hoeven and family, Rob Buchholz, Gary Walker, Pete Sigurtson, and unidentified. (Ray Erhardt photograph.)

At a 2009 Minot Y's Men's Rodeo performance, these two team ropers are working on both ends to get the steer tied up in the shortest amount of time. (Cowboy Images photograph.)

Nebraska all-around cowboy J.B. Lord does his best to get a hold of the steer at a 2009 Minot Y's Men's Rodeo performance. In this timed event, he needs to get the steer down on the ground as quickly as possible, with all four legs headed in the same direction. (Cowboy Images photograph.)

The header and heeler on this team-roping duo work on getting both ends tied at a 2009 Minot Y's Men's Rodeo performance. This rodeo is important to area children because the net proceeds go toward many projects that benefit the young. (Cowboy Images photograph.)

This bucking bronc is testing Ty Breuer, a young bronc rider from near Mandan. Raised in a rodeo family, Breuer rodeoed throughout high school and college years, participating on the Central Wyoming College rodeo team. He was the 2006–2008 NDHSRA bareback champion and went on to the NHSRA finals all three of those years. He then joined the PRCA, RRA, NPRA, and NDRA, traveling to rodeos throughout the country. Breuer won the 2010 ACRA championship.

Britany Fleck, of Mandan, is a champion barrel racer. After placing 17th in 2010, she qualified in the top 15 for her first trip to the WNFR in 2011. Fleck competes all year long across the country in order to build her winnings and qualify for the WNFR.

Lisa Lockhart, of Oral, South Dakota, runs the barrels at this 2009 Minot Y's Men's Rodeo, working toward the best time of all entrants. In barrel racing, riders want to make tight turns without downing barrels. (Cowboy Images photograph.)

Don Miller, of Raleigh, North Dakota, rides bareback broncs, as does his twin brother, Dan Miller. They travel to rodeos throughout the region.

A popular rodeo event for the children is "mutton bustin'." The young children hang on tight to the sheep's wool to get the best score and win a prize. For protection, they all wear vests and helmets. In this photograph, it is hard to tell if the child's face is showing fear or determination.

The pick-up men at the 2009 Minot Y's Men's Rodeo are ready to help this unidentified saddle-bronc rider during a rodeo performance. Their job is to get the rider safely off the bucking horse and onto the ground. After the rider is on the ground, the spectators can let him know how he did. (Cowboy Images photograph.)

Seven

Other Notable North Dakota Rodeos

A number of other North Dakota rodeos are previewed in this chapter, including the White Earth Valley Saddle Club Rodeo, North Dakota Winter Show Rodeo, Beulah Cowboys' Reunion Rodeo, Yucca Rodeo, and Blaisdell Rodeo. This photograph is of steer wrestling at the 1997 White Earth Valley Saddle Club Rodeo. The saddle club was organized in 1956. Stocks were sold at $25 per share to finance development of the rodeo arena. Stockholders were limited to 50 each, and the general member rate was $10 each.

Over the years, there have been many leaders in the White Earth Valley Saddle Club. In this photograph, taken at a White Earth Valley Rodeo, are just a few of them, including, from left to right, Arnold Krogen, Frank Crimmins, Ernest Ramberg, Carl Frisinger, and Bud Rice. Originally planned as just a roping club, the nearby Blaisdell Rodeo Club recommended that White Earth have a rodeo, as well.

Early in 1957, volunteers began building the arena and chutes on the east side of White Earth Valley Road. Bell Telephone donated the posts; the poles and boards came from Old Sanish. The first rodeo was held in July 1957, paying out $1,286 and bringing 3,000 spectators. Here is a shot of a bronc ride at the 1997 White Earth Valley Rodeo. By 1961, there were 5,000 spectators at the rodeo. The club also holds fun days, horse shows, steak fries, junior barrel-racing days, and trail rides.

The club and the rodeo have grown over the years, and improvements have been made to the rodeo grounds. A 500-seat covered grandstand with a concession stand underneath was completed in 1964, and events like the calf scramble and an "Almost Famous Shovel Race" were added to the rodeo. This photograph of the White Earth Valley Saddle Club was taken between the late 1950s and the early 1960s. Pictured are, from left to right, (first row) Mueller Marmon, Frank Crimmins, George Marmon, Jim Danks, Doug McGrady, Ernest Ramberg, Milt Danielson, and unidentified; (second row) Don Marmon, Terry Hjart, Arnold Krogen, Willard Hanson, Gilbert Raan, Martin Hegland, and Wally Chamley.

Angus Fox participated in an exciting saddle-bronc ride at the White Earth Valley Saddle Club Rodeo, placing second. In 1955, Fox was the NHSRA saddle-bronc runner-up champion in Harrison, Nebraska. He went on to capture 11 NDRA championship titles.

After construction of the North Dakota Winter Show Events Center was completed in 1963 on Valley City's Granger Hill, J.C. Stevenson produced the first NDRA Championship Finals in the new arena. The finals were hosted by the North Dakota Winter Show that began in 1937. The rodeo was sanctioned by the RCA in 1964, and, in 2011, it was inducted into the NDCHF. In the photograph at left, the cowboy gets out of the way as the bullfighter gets in between the bull and rider. This time, the bull's horns catch the bullfighter, and he is tossed in the air. Another bullfighter is ready to help.

This photograph shows Josh Tommeraus on a bull ride at a 2003 North Dakota Winter Show Rodeo performance. Bob Aber, from Beach, North Dakota, has been associated with the event since 1964, first as stock contractor and then as producer. Attracting top contestants and outstanding stock has allowed North Dakotans to enjoy professional rodeo and to follow the careers of cowboys and cowgirls as they progress toward world champion titles. (Doll Rodeo photograph.)

Rodeo stars such as Brad Gjermundson, Tex Appledoorn, and the famous North Dakota Six Pack have amazed the crowds that fill the 3,450 seats for rodeo performances, which are held in March each year. In this photograph, children get into the rodeo action at the North Dakota Winter Show PRCA Rodeo.

This rodeo is on par with rodeos in Cheyenne, Wyoming; Pendleton, Oregon; and Houston, Texas. Paul Weinberger, of Breien, North Dakota, is pictured participating in a bull ride at the 2003 Winter Show Rodeo. The Winter Show Rodeo specialty acts and visiting rodeo royalty, such as Brenda Lee (Bonogofsky) Pickett and Ashley Andrews-Alderson, have graced the arena every year since 1964. (Doll Rodeo photograph.)

This saddle bronc is giving the rider a tough ride at a recent North Dakota Winter Show Rodeo. However, he was disqualified for blowing (losing) a stirrup. The rodeo is an important draw at each annual North Dakota Winter Show.

This is a high-stepping saddle bronc at the North Dakota Winter Show Rodeo. The unidentified rider is doing his best to hold on until the eight-second buzzer blows.

This bull is kicking up the dirt while challenging the rider right out of the gate. Bull riding is possibly the most popular rodeo event; spectators seem to enjoy the dangerous aspects of it.

The bull is bucking hard to get rid of the rider, and the bullfighter is ready to help the rider if necessary. A bullfighter's role during a ride is to save the rider by distracting the bull and, at times, possibly risking his own life.

This photograph was taken at the Beulah Cowboys' Reunion Rodeo in 1929. The rodeo was popular every year for decades.

This photograph is of a horse race at the 1949 Beulah Cowboys' Reunion Rodeo. Racers are, from left to right, (first row) unidentified, Bea (Erickson) Murray (on Lars Handegard's horse), Phyllis (Murray) O'Neil, and Waldo Ost (on Baldie); (second row) Hubert Hafner (on Copper). (Lee Mohr photograph.)

South Dakota cowboy Howard Wanna is pictured riding a bucking bronc at a Beulah Rodeo. He eventually found his way to the Fort Berthold Indian Reservation, where he worked for area ranchers and participated in rodeos like Beulah, Sanish, Yucca, Minot, Killdeer, Elbowoods, Nishu, Independence, and Shell Creek. The NDCHF inducted Wanna in 2010. (Frank Fiske photograph.)

Horse racing was an important event at the Beulah Cowboys' Reunion Rodeo. This photograph includes Phyllis (Murray) O'Neil in front, riding bareback; Bea (Erickson) Murray in back on the left; and Donna Kranzel, in back on the right.

Joe Chase rides a saddle bronc at a Beulah Rodeo. As a member of the North Dakota Six Pack, Chase rodeoed across the country during the 1950s.

An unidentified rider tries out wild-cow riding at a Beulah Rodeo, while another cowboy watches. The town of Beulah is in the background. (Lee Mohr photograph.)

Pictured is Howard Wanna on Sky High at the 1928 Beulah Cowboys' Reunion Rodeo. In the 1920s, Wanna entered in bronc riding, bareback racing, horse races, and saddle-horse tug-of-war at Fort Berthold Indian Fairs. He participated before formal rodeo associations were organized—a time when all of the cowboys who were entered worked together to run a rodeo.

An unidentified cowboy commits to a bareback ride at the Beulah Cowboys' Reunion Rodeo. Whatever rodeo livestock a rider draws is all a matter of luck. The harder the animals buck, the better the score for riders, assuming they stay on for the required eight seconds.

This photograph was taken at the Beulah Cowgirls' Reunion Rodeo. The eight women on horseback are, from left to right, Bea Murray, Frances Erickson, Erogeline (Welsh) Erickson, Joyce (Murray) Herman, Cleo Herman, Mary Jaden, Myrtle (Erickson) LaRose, and Minnie Morman. (Frank Fiske photograph.)

Howard Wanna matches skills against this bareback bronc at the July 1927 Yucca Rodeo. Wanna had a successful yet short-lived rodeo career in the 1920s.

Ed Orgaard tried out wild-cow riding at the July 1927 Yucca Rodeo. Born in 1903, he ranched in Oliver County, North Dakota, most of his life and rodeoed throughout the state.

This 2008 photograph was taken at the Blaisdell Rodeo, held in June each year since 1956. Fans enjoy a great rodeo on Saturday and Sunday, topped off with a wild-horse race. (Rudlund photograph.)

In this photograph, Lee Selland participated in calf roping at the 1979 Blaisdell Rodeo. Raised in Steele, he competed in more than 650 rodeos throughout North Dakota, Montana, and beyond from 1963 to 2005. Over the years, he belonged to the RCA, RRA, MAPR, PRCA, USTRC, and the NDCHA. During his career, Selland won an impressive 22 championships around the country.

An unidentified rider challenges a bull at the Blaisdell Rodeo, while the bullfighter prepares to help him if necessary. The bull riders depend on the bullfighters for assistance.

Eight

North Dakota Rodeo Stars

This chapter includes some of North Dakota's best-known cowboys and cowgirls who have competed over the decades. Many of these rodeo stars have already been inducted into the NDCHF, and others may be included in the coming years. The photographs illustrate the range of rodeo events, including bronc riding, barrel racing, team roping, and bull riding. The above photograph shows the famous North Dakota Six Pack that traveled across the United States and Canada during the mid-1950s. Members of the Six Pack are, from left to right, Tom Tescher, Duane Howard, Dean Armstrong, Joe Chase, Jim Tescher, and Alvin Nelson. This image was taken at the Denver National Western Rodeo in the mid-1950s.

In 1998, four members of the North Dakota Six Pack were the first rodeo inductees into the NDCHF: Tom Tescher, Duane Howard, Jim Tescher, and Alvin Nelson. Joe Chase and Dean Armstrong were inducted in 1999. This photograph was taken at the August 1998 NDCHF induction ceremony in Medora. Pictured are, from left to right, Tom Tescher, Joe Chase, Duane Howard, Dean Armstrong, Jim Tescher, and Alvin Nelson.

Alvin Nelson is pictured riding the bareback-bronc Party Doll at the 1960 Ellensburg Rodeo. A South Dakota native, Nelson moved to North Dakota in 1953 and started rodeoing with Jim and Tom Tescher. Noted for his furious spurring style, his specialty was saddle bronc, but he also rode bareback broncs and bulls. (DeVere Helfrich photograph.)

Alvin Nelson rides Sorrel Top at Madison Square Garden in New York City in 1957. After buying a ranch near Grassy Butte in 1956, he continued pursuing his rodeo career. In 1957, at age 23, he became the first North Dakotan to win the RCA World Champion saddle-bronc buckle. He also won the saddle-bronc competition at the first Home On The Range Champions Ride in 1957.

In 1957, Alvin Nelson rode Piper at Harley Roth's Ox Yoke Rodeo in Nemo, South Dakota. In 1957, he was the runner-up RCA Saddle-bronc Champion and qualified for the NFR from 1960 to 1962 and in 1964 and 1966. Nelson won the NFR saddle-bronc riding average in 1961–1962. He rode professionally until the mid-1960s, winning and placing in the country's biggest rodeos. (DeVere Helfrich photograph.)

Joe Chase is pictured here on Jim Barnhart's No. 2 Whiz Bang. The photograph was taken at the 1956 Dickinson Match of Champions. From Elbowoods, North Dakota, Chase began rodeoing in high school, claiming his first rodeo title and buckle at the 1949 North Dakota State Saddle-bronc Championship at the Sanish rodeo grounds. He was inducted into the National Cowboy and Western Heritage Museum in 2009.

Joe Chase was the first of the Fort Berthold cowboys to leave the reservation for college. At Hardin-Simmons University in Abilene, Texas, he was the first North Dakotan to win national collegiate titles, claiming the ACRA saddle-bronc title in 1952 and 1953 and runner-up for all-around cowboy. He qualified for the NFR in 1960 and 1961. He also participated in bull riding and steer wrestling.

Duane Howard rode this Beutler Brothers' bull in Belle Fourche, South Dakota, in the late 1960s. A native of Minnewauken, North Dakota, he went on the pro-rodeo circuit after high school. In 1956, he was the RCA all-around runner-up champion and traveled the country in the 1950s and 1960s, riding bulls and saddle broncs. (Bob R. Robinson photograph.)

Duane Howard was the first North Dakotan to win a NHSRA title, which he did as the 1952 National Reserve Champion Bareback Rider. The two-time NFR qualifier rodeoed until he had a massive head injury while riding at Cheyenne Frontier Days in 1961. After learning to walk and talk again, he returned to bull riding. Here he rides Wild Man at a 1964 Billings, Montana, rodeo. Howard was inducted into the National Cowboy and Western Heritage Museum in 2009. (Allen photograph.)

Jim Tescher rides Detour at the Los Angeles Coliseum in 1961. One of the country's premier bronc riders in the 1950s and 1960s, the Sentinel Butte native gained a national reputation as an all-around cowboy, competing in saddle bronc, steer wrestling, and bull riding. (Mihne photograph.)

Jim Tescher rode Figure Four, a Fettig Brothers horse, at the NFR. He qualified for his first NFR in 1959 and was the first saddle-bronc average winner. He won the average again in 1963 and was second in the world saddle-bronc standings in 1964. He might have won the world title several times, but Tescher decided to leave the circuit and get back to ranching and family life.

Dean Armstrong was one of the North Dakota Six Pack who rodeoed across the country during the 1950s. Originally from Steele and later Sentinel Butte, North Dakota, Armstrong competed in rough stock and bulldogging events regionally and nationally during his rodeo career, bringing in all-around honors and prize money.

Dean Armstrong won the Miles City Bucking Horse Sale Rodeo and consistently ranked in the top 10 in saddle-bronc standings in the 1950s and 1960s. He placed at the nation's biggest rodeos and won 11 championship North Dakota RCA titles: six in bareback, two in saddle bronc, one in bull riding, and two in all-around. He also participated in calf roping and steer wrestling.

Tom Tescher rode Alkali at the Dickinson Match of Champions. Starting in Medora rodeos in 1943, he won the first State Saddle-bronc Riding Championship at Sanish in 1948 and 1950. Tescher competed in most events, winning most often in saddle bronc and steer wrestling. He was a 2009 National Cowboy and Western Heritage Museum inductee.

Tom Tescher is being bucked off Tea for Two at a 1964 Deadwood rodeo. He ranked in the top 10 of saddle-bronc riders from 1955 to 1958, qualifying for the 1959 NFR. He qualified again in 1960 but chose to be home for Christmas. Winning at the country's biggest rodeos, Tescher had a fierce riding style. He and brother Jim established the Home On The Range Champions Ride. (DeVere Helfrich photograph.)

Pete Fredericks secured the all-around championship at the NHSRA finals in 1955, winning the saddle-bronc and steer-wrestling events. He was a North Dakota high school champion in three events: bareback, saddle bronc, and steer wrestling. While at Dickinson State Teachers College, Fredericks helped organize the first rodeo team in 1958, the beginning of intercollegiate rodeo in North Dakota.

Pete Fredericks is pictured bulldogging at a 1972 New Town rodeo. In 1959, he rode at Madison Square Garden, placing in bareback, and he was named NIRA bareback and all-around champion. Fredericks won the bareback and saddle-bronc championship in 1961 and 1962, respectively. He went to the NFR three times, riding all 10 horses in 1961 and finishing as the number four bareback rider in the world.

Pete Fredericks rode Chicken Fry (Knight) in a 1972 Fort Worth, Texas, rodeo. Though no longer actively competing, he continued supporting rodeo by writing the National All-Indian Rodeo concept, approved by the PRCA, and was a member of the INFR commission. Fredericks received the Indian Rodeo Man of the Year Award in 1976. (Ferrell photograph.)

Angus Fox, a native of Elbowoods and graduate of Killdeer High School, remembers trailing cattle 50 miles over the Sanish Bridge to get the herd to a new area. He tamed and broke all of his own horses and began his rodeo career in 1950, participating in saddle bronc, bareback, team roping, bull riding, wild-horse racing, and calf roping.

Inducted into the NDCHF in 2009, Angus Fox was a member of the illustrious 1957–1958 Dickinson State Teachers College (DSTC) rodeo team that won the Rocky Mountain Regional Championship and went on to the College NFR. He belonged to the NDHSRA, NDRA, RCA, and GPIRA for many years. He won high school championships and 11 NDRA championships from 1954 to 1973.

The 1957–1958 DSTC rodeo team included, from left to right, Dale Hewson (advisor), Esley "Fox" Thornton, Pete Fredericks, Dale Jorgenson, and Franklin "Tex" Appledoorn. Three members of the team—Fredericks, Jorgenson, and Appledoorn—have since been inducted into the NDCHF.

Pictured is Henry "Almit" Breuer during a saddle-bronc ride at a 1960 Garrison rodeo. He started his rodeo career riding bareback horses and steers at nine years old. Breuer began competing in nearly every NDRA event in 1954, winning the saddle-bronc championship in 1954, 1955, 1960, and 1962 and winning all-around in 1960. Active in various rodeo and ranching organizations, he was inducted into the NDCHF in 2007.

Lawrence "Gene" Pedersen competed in saddle-bronc riding, roping, and steer wrestling. He is pictured steer wrestling at a 1956 Lewiston, Montana, rodeo. While attending Montana State College, he founded the first rodeo team in 1947 and tied for all-around cowboy. From 1946 to 1987, he participated in rodeos around North Dakota and Montana and, in the 1970s and 1980s, he added team roping and cow cutting. Pedersen won the 1952 Dickinson Match of Champions calf-roping and steer-wrestling events.

Joan (Hecker) Lennick is riding barrel patterns during the 1962 Miss Rodeo America horsemanship competition in Las Vegas. She won the NDHSRA barrel-racing title in 1956, three NDRA barrel-racing titles in 1959, 1961, and 1962, and ACRA barrel-racing and all-around titles in 1960. Lennick retired from barrel racing in 1965 and began judging rodeo queen pageants, horse shows, and the Miss Indian America Pageant.

John "Buzz" Fredericks Jr. is riding Automatic. Raised on the Fort Berthold Reservation, Fredericks started his rodeo career at age 14. At the 1956 ACRA finals, he was steer-wrestling champion and won third in bareback riding. He rodeoed throughout the country, competing at Madison Square Garden, the Pendleton Roundup, Calgary Stampede, and Cheyenne Frontier Days during the 1950s and 1960s.

John "Buzz" Fredericks Jr. rides a saddle bronc. He went on to enter bareback, saddle-bronc, and steer-wrestling events from 1947 to 1964. He won in RCA rodeos in North Dakota and finished ninth in the saddle-bronc standings in 1954 and fifth in 1956. Fredericks took up bull and steer riding and wild-horse racing in the 1950s, closing out his rodeo days in team-roping contests in the late 1960s and the 1970s. The NDCHF inducted him in 2010.

Bareback rodeo legend Wayne Herman is riding at a 1996 Cheyenne, Wyoming, rodeo. He won the world bareback title in 1992 and is a 10-time NFR qualifier. (Jennings Photography.)

Four-time world champion saddle-bronc rider Brad Gjermundson rode at the Home On The Range Champions Ride in the early 1990s. He won the NDHSRA team-roping championship in 1975, saddle-bronc championship in 1976 and 1977, and all-around in 1977. He competed in the NHSRA finals between 1975 and 1977. Joining the PRCA in 1980, he was rookie of the year and qualified for his first NFR in 1981. He went on to qualify for the NFR in 1982–1988 and again in 1994. He was inducted into the NDCHF in 2009.

Virginia Eck rounds the barrels at the Wing Rodeo. She is a former Miss Rodeo North Dakota, a four-time NDRA barrel-racing champion (1966, 1971–1973), and a founding NDCHF board member. Eck organizes barrel-racing competitions in North Dakota and leads a horse camp in Bismarck each June.

Maude (Kirk) Gullickson rode horses nearly every day until she was 73 years old, barrel racing throughout the Dakotas, Montana, and into Canada in the 1950s through 1970s. Gullickson won the State Cloverleaf title and the first NDRA Barrel Racing title in 1955. She was named Old Timers Rodeo Queen in 1982 and traveled to Las Vegas and Amarillo for the National Old Timers Finals in 1983. She was inducted into the NDCHF in 2011.

Jim Johnston is on No. T-25 in a 1966 Bowman, North Dakota, rodeo. He grew up around rodeo, breaking and training horses and working with the Fettig Rodeo Company of Killdeer. He entered his first rodeo in the late 1950s. His experience working for the Fettigs gave him the opportunity to see the nation's top cowboys performing and to also compete against them. He was inducted into the NDCHF in 2004. (Rabun photograph.)

Bruce Northrop worked with Fettig Brothers Rodeo and started competing in saddle-bronc, bareback, calf-roping, and wild-horse races. In 1968, he went to jackpot ropings, bringing home his first buckle in 1955. He earned many saddles, buckles, and money prizes during his 50-year rodeo career. In 2009, he placed first and second at the World Series of Team Roping qualifiers. He competed in the 2009 and 2010 WSTR finals and was inducted into the NDCHF in 2011.

Darrell Hermanson, of Kathryn, North Dakota, won the NDRA bull-riding championship in 1972 and 1973. He competed in bull riding and was the bull-riding champion at the 1973 NHSRA finals in Ogden, Utah. (J. Fain Photograph Associates.)

A 2002 NDCHF inductee, Dale Jorgenson qualified for the 1966 NDRA finals. He began his rodeo career competing in high school and non-RCA rodeos. He was the 1956 NDHSRA bareback and all-around champion, but he was unable to attend the NHSRA finals after a near drowning accident. His first NDRA championship came in 1957 in bareback riding, and he was the first non-RCA cowboy to ever win the North Dakota all-around saddle. (Rabun photograph.)

Since 1970, Jerry Weinberger, of Breien, was a four-time NDRA bull-riding champion. He is pictured riding J.C. Stevenson's No. 25 Big John. The toughest bull he remembers riding was Old Yellow Jacket at the 1961 Grant County Fair when he was a high school freshman.

This photograph is of Wilfred "Sonny" Ehr Jr. at a 1965 Great Falls, Montana, rodeo. He won two NDHSRA calf-roping titles in the late 1950s and the 1959 NHSRA calf-roping championship at Lewistown, Montana. Ehr also received the Waldo Vangness Memorial Trophy at the NHSRA finals.

Pictured is Sonny Ehr at a 1967 Palm Springs rodeo. While at Oklahoma State University, he competed in the NIRA's Southwest Region and won the 1962 NIRA national championship in steer wrestling. He repeated this accomplishment in 1963, while competing for the University of Arizona. Ehr was inducted into the NDCHF in 2001. (Foxie photograph.)

Frank Whitecalfe honed his roping skills while team roping with his dad, Oscar Whitecalfe. Starting in 1970, Frank participated in bareback riding, team roping, calf roping, and steer wrestling, qualifying for the 1970 and 1971 NHSFR. He won his first team-roping title in 1974. In 1977, he won the world champion Indian steer-wrestling title, along with many all-around, calf-roping, and team-roping championships in the RRA and GPIRA during the 1980s and 1990s.

Howard Wanna is pictured here on Crow-hi-in at the Sanish Rodeo. He rodeoed around North Dakota, especially on the Fort Berthold Indian Reservation, during the 1920s. Wanna's rodeo skills were captured often by photographers Frank Fiske and Leo Harris. (Photograph by L.D. Harris.)

Rodeo participant Reuben DeCamp is seen here on Smoky Jo. He rode in the Mandan Rodeo in 1925 and competed in the Almont, Carson, Sanish, Weekes Ranch, and Yucca rodeos. He was inducted into the NDCHF in 2010.

An NDCHF inductee in 2002, George Bruington began rodeoing in 1925 and, for 73 years, he competed in bareback, saddle bronc, team tying, calf roping, and bulldogging. He was a pick-up man, a clown, a stock contractor, and a rodeo judge. By the late 1960s, he had built up his herd to become one of the NDRA's top contractors. Many of his horses won NDRA and NFR awards.

George Defender, from the Standing Rock Reservation, was inducted into the NDCHF in 2001. He started competing in North Dakota rodeos by 1914. From 1918 to 1923, he competed across the United States and Canada in bareback, bulldogging, calf roping, relay races, wild-horse races, wild-cow milking, and buffalo riding. He was a final contender for world championship all-around cowboy honors and was considered one of the toughest bronc riders of his time.

Scott Gore is riding at a July 1915 rodeo in Watford City. A South Dakota native, Gore became a nationally known rodeo champion and rancher. He rode in Buffalo Bill's Wild West Show in Europe and became a North Dakota state saddle-bronc champion. Gore won championships in Glendive, Montana, and Watford City and was inducted into the NDCHF in 2002.

A 2000 NDCHF inductee, Louis Pelissier is pictured on Sambo. He decided at a young age that he wanted to be a cowboy and started working on Medora area ranches at age 15. By 17, he was breaking wild horses. From 1916 through the 1960s, Pelissier was best known in rodeo circles as a top-notch pick-up man. He enjoyed team roping in the 1960s. (Presthus photograph.)

Reuben DeCamp is riding Heart River Girl. His rodeo career was short-lived because of his early death in an October 2, 1930, fire. He left a wife and young son.

This is a wonderful shot of Bob Christophersen steer wrestling (or "bulldogging"). He began bulldogging in 1959 and, in college, competed in steer wrestling, calf roping, and ribbon roping from 1969 to 1973, attending the National Intercollegiate Finals from 1970 to 1973. Christophersen got his RCA card in 1967 and qualified for the NFR in steer wrestling from 1971 to 1975 and also in 1977. He was the Cheyenne Frontier Days Rodeo and NDRA average champion in 1996.

Walter Neuens is on Steel Dust at a 1928 rodeo. A Medora native and 2004 NDCHF inductee, he began his rodeo career at 14 with a Wild West show. After marrying NDCHF founding president Evelyn Connell, he competed in area rodeos and assisted with rodeos, horse shows, and 4-H events. They operated the Ferris Store in Medora and produced events at the Medora Ranchorama.

Lyndon "Frank" Marshall rides a bull at an unidentified area rodeo. At a young age, he rode a bull at a Montana rodeo. Marshall won and rode again the next day. On the rodeo circuit, he entered saddle-bronc, bareback, and bulldogging events, competing at rodeos across the United States and Canada. In 1942, he was the fourth best bull rider in the world and the 25th best all-around cowboy. He was inducted into the NDCHF in 2003.

Ralph Klein grew up on a combination farm and ranch, and he knew horses. While with the US Army in the South Pacific, he belonged to the roping club and participated in Sunday rodeos, along with other soldiers. Back in North Dakota, he joined the Bismarck Horse Club and was a member of the NDRA and RCA. He rodeoed around the Dakotas and in Montana, winning the state calf-roping championship in 1950.

In this c. 1962 photograph, 2010 NDCHF inductee Lee Selland is pictured calf roping. In 1970, he claimed an unprecedented achievement, winning four NDRA championship saddles that season. He won in calf roping, steer wrestling, team roping, and all-around.

Dale Jorgenson is pictured on Smokie at the 1972 New Salem rodeo. Jorgenson was on the first DSTC rodeo team in 1957–1958, finishing third in the NIRA bull-riding standings in 1958. In 1968, Jorgenson competed at a four-state bronc ride, taking second in saddle bronc and bareback. He earned 14 NDRA championships and other wins from 1957 to 1975. Jorgenson also enjoyed team roping.

Inducted into the NDCHF in 2005, Alvin "Gabby" Gabbert of New Salem started raising registered Quarter horses in 1950. In his indoor arena, he trained horses and held roping and horsemanship clinics. From the 1950s–1970s, Gabbert was a champion calf roper and team roper. From 1953–1969, he showed performance horses throughout the United States and Canada, winning many trophies and buckles.

In 1955, Jerry Osterhout, of Sentinel Butte, rode this bull at the Seventh Annual NHSRA finals in Harrison, Nebraska. He started rodeoing by riding cows and became the 1955 NDHSRA bull-riding champion. He qualified twice for the NHSRA finals and began competing in amateur rodeos in 1954. (James Cathey photograph.)

Inducted into the NDCHF in 2001, Sonny Ehr was the 1976 team-roping champion. In 1978, he was the steer-wrestling champion, claiming all-around cowboy honors at the 1978 circuit finals. He was the only North Dakotan at the NFR in 1970, qualifying in steer wrestling and ending the year 11th in the nation.

Inducted into the NDCHF in 2003, Franklin "Tex" Appledoorn is calf roping at a 1967 Montana rodeo. He competed on the first DSTC rodeo team in 1957–1958. At the college NFR, Appledoorn won calf-roping and steer-wrestling titles. He earned state calf-roping titles in 1956–1958 and 1960–1968; steer-wrestling titles in 1959, 1960, 1964, and 1967; and all-around championships in 1965, 1967, and 1968.

Jim Johnston is pictured bull riding in a 1966 Williston rodeo. During his rodeo career, he also competed in steer wrestling. He won a series of 12 NDRA/RCA championships and was inducted into the NDCHF in 2004. (Rabun photograph.)

Jim Johnston is seen bareback riding in Williston around 1969. Johnston also worked in all areas of the arena—sorting horses, pulling flanks, competing, driving trucks, and being a pick-up man. Johnston rodeoed across the region from 1950 to the late 1970s. (Rabun photograph.)

Lee Selland was a NDRA all-around and roping champion. He also trained countless champion horses for the rodeo arena, and many of his students became rodeo champions. Selland was active in a number of horse-related organizations. He also produced and managed rodeos, taught countless rodeo schools, and judged horse clinics.

Lee Selland was steer wrestling at Strasburg in the mid-1980s, with his son Terry Selland as hazer. In 1975, Selland was named the North Dakota Cowboy of the Year and was chosen by the NDRA and the state highway department tourism bureau for the state's "roughrider" travel promotion.

An unidentified cowboy looks for a successful steer-wrestling run. The hazer is important in keeping the steer running straight as it comes out of the chute so the steer wrestler can catch up and get a good angle for reaching the steer.

Shaun Stroh, of Dickinson, makes North Dakota proud at the PRCA National Circuit Finals Rodeo. He rodeoed full-time, traveling to as many as 120 rodeos a year throughout the United States and Canada. Stroh qualified for the NFR in 2004–2005 and 2008–2010. At the 2008 NFR, he placed 12th in the world standings. (WNFR photograph.)

Dusty Hausauer is pictured in a saddle-bronc ride at the 2008 Ponoka (Alberta) Stampede. A Dickinson native, Hausauer won the Canadian saddle-bronc championship in Edmonton, Alberta, and went on to finish ninth in the world standings at the WNFR in Las Vegas. He competed in saddle bronc in North Dakota and Canada, traveling to more than 100 rodeos each year. (Copeman photograph.)

Nine

North Dakota Rodeo Livestock

The photograph shows Double Jeopardy at the 1976 NFR. Belonging to Bob Aber, the steed's rodeo career started in Forsyth, Montana, and went on to the NFR for eight consecutive years, from 1976 to 1983. He placed first at the 1977 NFR, third in 1978 and 1979, and was inducted into the NDCHF in 2010. High-quality rodeo livestock is key to a successful rodeo and makes a difference in where the cowboys and cowgirls place in the event standings. (James Fain photograph.)

Jim Tescher is riding Red Pepper at a 1963 Deadwood rodeo. An NDCHF inductee in 2008, the saddle bronc was a red sorrel gelding purchased by the Fettig Brothers in the late 1950s. He was a consistent bucking horse, performing well in any and all conditions. Selected for the NFR for 11 years, he appeared in 20 performances. Cowboys placed in the top four on him 15 times. He was the top saddle bronc at the Deadwood Days of '76 Rodeo.

Old Fitzgerald, owned by Linton horse buyer John Steen, does his job at a 1948 Steen Rodeo. A Percheron-cross work horse, he was first bucked at the Saturday Indian rodeos near Fort Yates. He was hauled to rodeos across North Dakota during the 1950s and 1960s. Only six or seven of the cowboys drawing Old Fitzgerald made the whistle during the more than 10 years he bucked in North Dakota. He was inducted into the NDCHF in 2001.

Harley May drew Old Fitzgerald at the 1956 Dickinson Match of Champions. Dressed in a saddle and flank strap, he could throw top cowboys. Otherwise, he was amazingly gentle. The horse was more than 20 years old when he was retired, probably to a pasture in the Cannon Ball area. For rough-stock events, the horses and bulls are judged on a possible 50 points for the ride, and the cowboys can receive 50 points. (DeVere Helfrich photograph.)

NDCHF inductee Whiz Bang was born in 1948 on the Walt Neuens ranch north of Medora. His rodeo career began in Belfield in 1954, when Bubb Nunn drew him for a bareback ride. With Whiz Bang's reputation for being a very rank horse, riders were quickly bucked off him. This photograph shows Tom Tescher leaving Whiz Bang at a 1956 Dickinson Match of Champions rodeo.

Though nearly impossible to make a qualified ride on him, Whiz Bang gained immortal fame at the 1956 Dickinson Match of Champions when Joe Chase drew him and got it done. This photograph shows J.D. McKenna losing the battle against Whiz Bang at the 1956 Dickinson rodeo. Casey Tibbs bought him in 1960, and the bucking horse was inducted into the NDCHF in 2004. (Osborn's Studio.)

This photograph shows Little Yellow Jacket, often called the "most famous bull in the world," at the 2003 NFR. Bred and raised by the Joe Berger family of Mandan, he was hauled to bull-riding events all over the country and was named the PBR World Champion Bucking Bull from 2002 to 2004. By the end of 2004, he had been ridden only 14 times in 90 attempts. He bucked for the last time in 2005 in Bismarck and was inducted into the NDCHF in 2006. (Andy Watson photograph.)

Old Shep is shown bucking at the Home On The Range Champions Ride. Owned by Bob Aber, the sorrel gelding bucked in 15 consecutive NFRs from 1970 to 1984. He was named top saddle bronc at the 1975 NFR and voted twice as second best at the NFR. Old Shep also earned the Home On The Range Champions Ride's best bronc honors five times. He was inducted into the NDCHF in 2000.

Casey Tibbs rode Figure Four at the 1956 Dickinson Match of Champions. Born in the late 1910s near Killdeer, this champion horse was sold to Nick Fettig and became part of the Fettig bucking-horse string His first rodeo performance was in 1952 at the Killdeer Mountains Roundup Rodeo, with Duane Howard on his back. Figure Four was inducted into the NDCHF in 2002.

Anchors Aweigh was raised near Blaisdell and bucked in bareback- and saddle-bronc events in the Blaisdell NDRA Rodeo in 1971. He was purchased by the Figure Four Rodeo Company and dominated the saddle-bronc riding scene in North Dakota for more than 20 years. Anchors Aweigh was named the NDRA Saddle Bronc of the Year several times and, in 1982, he was named the Most Outstanding Saddle Bronc horse in Denver. He was inducted into the NDCHF in 2008.

Ten

North Dakota Rodeo Entertainers

What is a rodeo without entertainment? Some would say it would not be a rodeo at all. This chapter honors just a few notable rodeo entertainers: clowns, bullfighters, trick riders, and others. This photograph is of Steven W. "Steve" Tomac, who started his rodeo career at a young age near Meadow, South Dakota. When a clown got laughs from the crowd, Tomac decided that he would like to do that. He got his start in July 1971 at a Raleigh rodeo and made a final appearance at the Mandan Rodeo in 2005. He was inducted into the NDCHF in 2008, and his barrel is now on display at the NDCHF.

Steve Tomac's awards and recognition include North American Rodeo Commission Finals Barrelman in 1981, Badlands Circuit Finals Barrelman nearly every year from 1985 to 2002, and NFR runner-up barrelman and Dodge National Circuit Finals Barrelman in 1990. He was a bullfighter from 1971 to 1980 and a barrelman and contract specialty act from 1975 to 2004, mostly in the upper Midwest. From 1983 to 2001, he worked 40 to 50 PRCA performances a year in seven states.

This unidentified cowgirl is entertaining the rodeo spectators with her trick-riding routine at a late-1940s Mandan Rodeo. Considerable training for both the rider and the horse takes place before a real performance. (Bob Luck photograph.)

Entertaining the rodeo audience, Ray Ramsey shows off his popular trick-riding stunt, the Roman standing jump, at a late-1940s Mandan Rodeo. (Doubleday photograph.)

Kathleen (Ray) Barger gets her horse to do some tricks to entertain the rodeo audience. Barger grew up on the family ranch near Medora and performed in the 1930s and 1940s. Her trick-riding career began when two rodeo performers came to their ranch and taught her and her younger brother to trick ride. She and her brother performed together, and individually, throughout North Dakota and Minnesota.

Dick Woodbury, from Carson, became interested in rodeo and bullfighting when he was young, and he has been pursuing it since then. He travels around the region and beyond for his bullfighting. Woodbury participated in the 2006 Northern Plains Rodeo Association Finals in Bismarck.

Marvin Klein, from Carson, is pictured clowning at amateur rodeos in the 1960s, earning his RCA card in 1970. He clowned, fought bulls, and promoted rodeo in at least 17 states in 1979 and 1980. (Fain Photographic, Ltd., photograph.)

Marvin Klein helps a bull rider by distracting the bull. It looks like a close call. Bullfighting is a serious and sometimes dangerous occupation. Klein was named the PRCA Badlands circuit bullfighter of the year in 1979 and 1980. (Ray Erhardt photograph.)

INDEX

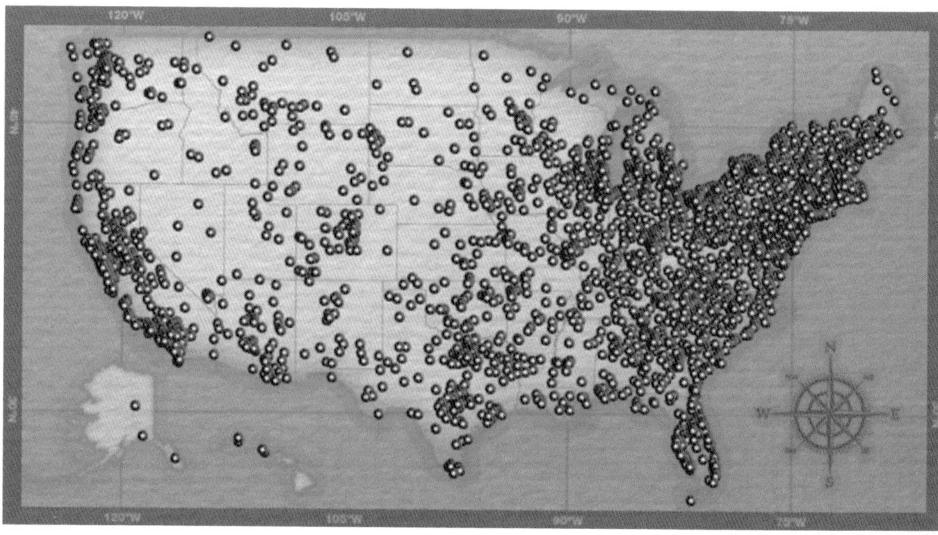